LITTLE BEAR

and
Other Native American Animal Tales

RETOLD BY CHEYENNE CISCO

Celebration Press
Pearson Learning Group

Contents

LITTLE BEAR

An Inuit Tale

Up on the ice at the top of the world, life is not easy. During the long, cold winters, the wind blows sharply and the snow falls heavily. The days are short, and food is not easy to come by. But during the long, dark nights, the stars spin brightly overhead, and the people always care for one another.

Long ago an old woman lived in a simple hut at the edge of a village there. The woman could not provide food for herself. She could do little more than gather snow to melt for fresh water. However, the hunters were kind and looked after her. When they were successful, they gave her bear meat or whale blubber, and so she lived on.

One day the hunters brought something different to the woman's hut. The youngest stood in the doorway and held something up in his hand. He spoke to her with respect. "Look, Old Friend! Do you want it?" he asked. It was a ball of dirty white fur, a half-frozen polar bear cub whose mother was nowhere to be found.

The woman took the tiny cub gently in her hands. Oh, yes, she wanted it. She wanted it very badly. You see, she had no children or other family, and she was often lonely. It would be good to have a living creature to care for and to keep her company during the long winters at the top of the world.

The old woman held the cub close and warmed it and sang to it. When the cub opened its eyes, she rejoiced. She dried its dripping fur, gave it water to drink, and fed it from her own store of blubber and meat. On the floor of her hut, she made the small creature a bed of the warmest sealskins.

The bear cub was like a puppy, full of love and mischief. It poked its nose here and there and explored its new home. The old woman cared for it as she would her own child and it brought her much happiness. She called the cub Little Bear.

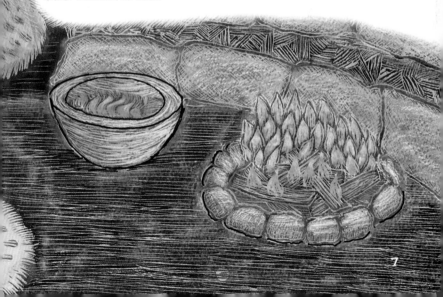

Little Bear was not
little for long, though.
Soon his feet were the size
of snowshoes.

The village children came to
play with him every day. He raced
them up the hills and then rolled
back down like a giant snowball.
When he grew bigger, he pulled the
children across the ice on homemade
sleds. Little Bear was gentle and always
took care not to use his claws. Still, he was
so big that he would sometimes snap a child's
toy harpoon, just by touching it—and he
wasn't finished growing yet.

After a time the children of the village grew frightened of Little Bear because he was so enormous. They no longer came to play. Instead, their fathers came to the old woman's hut.

"Old Friend," said one of the men, "let us take Little Bear hunting with us. He can help us catch seals at their blowholes."

So Little Bear became a hunter. He was fast and strong and could catch even the largest seal with a single swipe of his paw.

When the weather was bad and snow painted the sky white, the men had to stay home, but not Little Bear. He went hunting alone and brought back seals enough for the whole village. Oh, times were good then; bellies were full.

But the good times could not last forever. One night on their way home, the hunters stopped again at the old woman's hut. "Old Friend," they said, "a harpoon missed your bear by only the width of a mitten today. Hunters from the village to the west were stalking him."

You see, people from all the other villages had heard of the giant bear with the perfect, thick white fur. The best hunters had vowed to kill him for his hide.

After that, the old woman could not rest. She was fearful and felt her heart squeeze inside her chest each time she saw Little Bear go out to hunt. Finally she could stand it no longer.

The woman was filled with sadness, but she knew what she must do: She must send Little Bear away. But first she mixed lamp soot with her tears and smeared it on the bear's snow-white side. Perhaps if the people saw him again, they would know him by this mark and not harm him.

"Humans are humans and animals are animals," she told him. "We can stay together no longer. Go now. Go back to your own kind, far away, out where the ice floes drift. You will be safe and happy there."

The bear seemed to understand. He licked the woman's hand and left her hut. Slowly he walked north and disappeared from sight. The old woman stood outside her door and stared at his tracks in the snow until night swallowed up the sky.

Little Bear was gone, but for all her life, whenever times were hard and the men of the village could not hunt, the old woman found good fresh meat lying outside her door. And far to the north, even today, when the bears are out on the ice, people say there is always one bear, larger than all the others, with a black spot on one side.

Coyote and Old Man Rock

A Story from the Sioux Tribe

One day, Coyote was walking along, all done up in his best clothes like a fine and fancy present. He was wearing his best deerskin shirt, his best beaded moccasins, and his best bear claw necklace. On top of it all, he wore his richest, most colorful blanket. In fact, Coyote wasn't so much walking as he was strutting. He was on his way to a big powwow.

"Ah, I am one handsome fellow," he said to himself.

The way to the powwow was flat as a griddle, and hot as one, too. There wasn't a cloud in the sky. The sun beat down without a stop, and there were no trees to provide shade.

Soon Coyote felt like he was boiling inside those fancy clothes, steaming like an ear of corn in a pot. He wanted to shed some of them. He spotted a large boulder beside the path and strolled over to it.

Now coyote was very clever. He always had a plan. "Hello there, Old Man Rock," Coyote said. "You look awfully warm, sitting out here in the blazing sun. I think I'll help you out." Coyote took off his blanket and laid it over the rock. "There you go," he said. "Take this beautiful blanket to shade you, Father Rock. No need to thank me." Coyote grinned. "I'm just a generous fellow."

17

It was a long way to the big powwow.
Coyote kept walking. Before he knew it, the
air started to chill. Dark clouds piled up
overhead like dirty sheep. Drizzle fell, then
the drizzle turned to rain, and the rain turned
to sleet. It didn't take long for Coyote to
wheel around and run right back to that rock.

"Hello again!" Coyote said. "Remember
me, Old Man Rock? I'm the one who
loaned you that lovely, warm blanket. You
don't need it anymore. Let me take it for
you. It's probably getting soggy anyhow."
He whisked the blanket off the rock
and around his own shoulders.

Ahhh, it felt good to be
warm again. Once again
Coyote headed toward
the powwow.

19

Coyote trekked along without a care for a while. Maybe he heard a little grumble in the air. Maybe he sensed a little rumble far off in the distance. If he did, he ignored it.

He ignored it, that is, until he couldn't ignore it anymore. Soon that grumble turned into a groan, and the groan turned into a growl. And that rumble turned into a racket, and the racket turned into a roar. When Coyote looked back, that big boulder, that Old Man Rock, was rolling right toward him!

Now Coyote surely could run. He was quick as lightning. He cut left; he dashed right. He splashed across a river basin and scurried up a slope trying to outrun Old Man Rock. He zigzagged between some trees, hoping to throw him off course. But wherever he ran, and no matter how fast he ran, that boulder was right behind him.

Then it happened. Coyote tripped over the edge of his fine blanket—oof! splat!—and that big old rock rolled right over him. Coyote was knocked flat as a pancake. Old Man Rock didn't even slow down though; that boulder kept right on rolling. It turned in a big circle and then headed back for its place by the path. Coyote's rich, fine, colorful blanket was stuck tightly to its side.

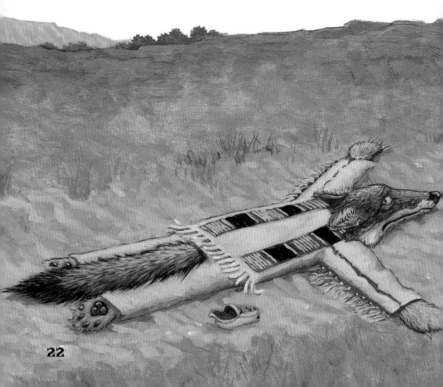

At first Coyote couldn't move. He looked like a furry, old rug, lying there all flattened out. As Old Man Rock rolled away, Coyote heard him call out, "Remember this, my good friend. It is not gracious to take back a gift that one has presented to another. What is given is given."

Coyote managed to get up after a while. He dusted himself off and even stumbled on toward that powwow. He's a stubborn one, you know. But he never forgot Old Man Rock, and he never quite got his shape back. That's why every coyote, ever since, has been as skinny as a split-rail fence.

Little Turtle's Raid

An Iroquois Folk Tale

Every Iroquois mother tells every Iroquois child how Earth rests on Big Turtle's back. It has been that way since time began. Now most people think it is fine and noble for Big Turtle to be holding up the world. Even so, there was once a little turtle who was dissatisfied. He wished the reputation of turtles were even greater.

Over on Flat Pond, Little Turtle didn't do much of anything, except chew on leaves, float on his back, and think. What he thought was that no turtle, in all of history, had ever done anything really important. After all, had any turtle had a great adventure? Had any turtle performed a truly brave deed? Had any turtle ever led a war party?

Nobody else seemed to be doing anything about the situation, so Little Turtle decided he would have to be the one to bring glory to the turtles.

"I'll be the first warrior turtle—the strongest leader and the wisest chief the turtle tribe has ever had," he thought. "I'll start with a big raid to show how brave I am."

Early the next morning Little Turtle got out his canoe and paddled off upstream, singing to himself:

I am on a raid.
I am on a raid.
I will be the bravest turtle
The world has ever had.

The animals along the shore asked Little Turtle where he was going. They all wished him well on his great adventure.

Now it was hard work paddling upstream, and Little Turtle wasn't exactly sure whose camp to raid, but when his arms got tired and he saw a lodge by the side of the stream, he figured that was good enough. He climbed out of his canoe and hid in the bushes by the water. There he planned his daring deed.

Three young sisters lived together in the lodge. Soon they awoke and began their morning chores. When the oldest came to the river to get water, Little Turtle gave his loudest, most blood-curdling war cry, but the girl just laughed and pushed him over on his back with her foot. When the next oldest came to wash her face, upside-down Turtle snapped at her, but she poked him with a stick. When the youngest girl came, she leaned close to look at Little Turtle. He grabbed her big toe in his strong jaws and held on for dear life.

"Aieeeeee!" cried the girl. She shook her foot but could not get him off.

When the other sisters heard the screams, they rushed to see what was the matter.

"Quick! Throw him in the fire!" said the oldest sister. "Quick! Dump him in the stream!" said the middle sister.

31

Turtle had to think fast. "Yes! All right! Put me in the fire!" said Turtle without loosening his jaws. "But not the water! Please! No! I'll sink like a stone. I'll drown in there!"

Turtle begged and pleaded. So, of course, the sisters dragged him into the water as fast as they could. Turtle let go then and dove for the bottom of the stream.

So that is how Little Turtle came to see he was not cut out to be a great warrior chief. However, he wasn't done thinking, and the more he thought about it, the more satisfied he was just to be a little turtle.

Maybe no turtle had ever gained fame as a leader of warriors, but the whole world does rest on the back of a turtle. Surely that makes turtles pretty important.

Stubborn Skunk

A Legend from the Salish Indians of the Northwest

Long, long ago the Star People wandered the sky, roaming wherever they pleased. One night, while their husbands were off fishing, the Star Women decided to cook a big batch of camas lily roots for the evening meal. They searched the clouds for the plumpest, juiciest plants. They hunted on the far side of the moon for nice, flat rocks to place in the fire. They dug a deep fire pit and ran here and there and back again, gathering sticks to feed the flames.

Soon the fire blazed brightly and the pit was ready for cooking. The women carefully placed the plump roots they had gathered among the hot rocks. As the roots began to steam, their fragrance filled the air. Mmm! What a sweet, delicious smell blew all around the heavens then!

When Skunk got a whiff of that delectable aroma, he put his pointy nose up in the air and followed it, all the way to the Star Women's cook fire.

Skunk marched right up to the fire circle. There was no need for him to sneak; everyone knew what would happen if someone tried to stop him.

A young woman saw him first. "Look out!" she yelped. "It's Mr. Stink!" She ran and hid behind her lodge. Other women screeched and grabbed their children and followed her.

But not all of the women ran away. A few stayed by the cook fire. "I worked hard for this meal," said one woman. "No stinker is going to take it away from me."

"That's right. It's ours. I don't care how I smell," the others agreed.

Skunk was amazed. No one had ever been
bold enough to challenge him like this
before. Skunk was also very hungry. He
hadn't eaten in awhile, and he was always
on the lookout for an easy meal. His mouth
watered; his belly growled. All he could
think about was a nice big helping of sweet
steamed roots. He really wanted to take his
share of that delicious food.

"Maybe if I'm still, they'll forget all about me, or maybe they'll grow tired and go away," he thought. He stood motionless and waited. Skunk stared across the fire at the Star Women. The Star Women stared back at Skunk. No one budged; they were all too stubborn to give in.

So they stand to this day. If you look up at the sky on a clear night, you will see them. Those Star Women are grouped around their cook fire, which still burns brightly, and nearby is the outline of Skunk, still hoping for a chance to grab an easy meal.

Raven Makes the Tides

A Tsimshian Legend from
the Pacific Northwest

Things were not always as they
are now, children. Long ago the
oceans were quiet and the tides did
not wash in and out.

The sea stayed high up on the
shore. Seaweed and clams, crabs and
other good things to eat were
hidden deep under the water.
People who lived near the shore
often had empty bellies.

One day Raven was soaring high above the shore. "This isn't right," she said. "The sea has more than enough. People should not go hungry when there is such an abundance of food that could nourish them."

Back then, Raven knew well what is fair and what is not. Maybe she does today, too.

Raven spread her wings and let the wind carry her like a big black kite, up, up along the shoreline until she came to the end of the world. There she found a string that led to a house on top of a cliff. Inside the house was a very old woman who held the string tightly in her hand. That string was the tide line. The old woman was holding that tide in as far as it could go!

Raven had a plan. She stood in the old woman's doorway.

"Greetings, Mother," Raven said. "Thank you for the clams; they were delicious."

"What clams?" the old woman demanded.

"Why, the clams I picked up on the shore where the tide was low," said Raven.

"That can't be!" cried the woman. "Let me see!" As she came to the door to look out, Raven flapped her feathers furiously. Sand blew up into the woman's face and she began to scrub fiercely at her eyes to get the dirt out. When she did, she dropped the tide line and the tide rushed out, leaving clams and crabs and other good things to eat along the shore.

Raven flew down to the beach. All along
the shore, people were gathering the good
food the sea had delivered. They gathered
mussels, clams, and crabs. Then they ate until
they could eat no more and thanked Raven
for what she had done. Raven, having eaten
her fill, returned to the old woman's house.

"Raven, you tricked me!" the woman declared. She rubbed and rubbed at her face. "Help me get this sand out of my poor old eyes."

"I will help you," said Raven, "but only if you promise to let go of the tide line twice a day from now on."

"All right, I will do it," said the woman. "I will release the line two times every day. You have my word."

Raven flapped her wings furiously to blow the sand away, and the woman was able to see again. From that day to this, the old woman has kept her promise. That is why twice a day the tide rises and twice a day the tide falls. Thanks to Raven there are always good things to eat along the shore.